RUTH READY

IN BUSINESS
The Basics of Business

KITTY ARCENEAUX

RUTH READY IN BUSINESS
Copyright © 2021 by ELEVATE'HER UP LLC

All rights reserved. No part of this book may be reproduced or transmitted in any form or by any means without written permission from the author.

ISBN: 9798496850087

The views stated herein are those of the author alone and should not be taken as expert counsel. This information is strictly for informational purposes only.

Introduction

Starting a business might seem to be overwhelming at times, but if this is a desire that you have in your heart take the necessary steps to get it done.

It is extremely important to align yourself with the people who care about you, your vision, and your business. One thing I found is that you cannot do it alone. The village is still important when you're trying to get to the next level in life and in business.

I hope that this book will motivate you to not only get it started, but to get it done and flourish in your business as G-d intended.

Beloved, I pray that in every way you may succeed and prosper and be in good health just as your soul prospers.

Ruth tells Naomi, "I'm going to work; I'm going out to glean among the sheaves, following anyone in whose eyes I may find favor."

I bet you never read the book of Ruth and thought about business. Well, if you really look at it from a different standpoint you would see her as an independent contractor or even an entrepreneur. In addition, I am sure you never thought that the book of Ruth could change the way you do business. The first thing you want to do is make sure you see G-d as the owner of your business, the decision-maker, and the problem-solver.

The book of Ruth gets to a point where they talk about gleaning and gleaning defined is *extract (information) from various sources, collect gradually bit by bit and gather after a harvest.*

This lets us know what we should consider before starting a business. We should gather our information making sure we have all the facts for our product or service. Know who our customers are, make sure we have all our paperwork in order, what our prices are and what we are offering. Once we have everything in order and ready to do business, we can then see a harvest.

The book of Ruth tells the incredible story of G-d's faithfulness through both economic lack and wealth; we see the hand of G-d at work clearly in labor, management, and creativity. Throughout everything, G-d's faithfulness creates opportunities for abundant work, and it is our dependability on G-d that brings the blessing of provision and surety to everyone involved.

I read once that the events in the book of Ruth took place at the time of the festival of the barley harvest when the connection between G-d's blessing and human labor was celebrated. This lets us know that development, creativity, and production is an expansion of G-d's work in our business, and G-d's blessing on our work is linked to G-d's ability to provide.

Well, my question to you is this: **Are you Ruth Ready in Business?** Let us look at a few things that are involved in being Ruth Ready in business.

INTEGRITY- We are living in a time where integrity is often compromised for the sake of worldly gain. Despite this, the book of Ruth reminds us how G-d honors integrity. Ruth decided to follow Naomi instead of going back to what was comfortable and familiar. It was that decision of loyalty and accountability that set Ruth apart and allows us to see her character and integrity. Ruth's loyalty was evident in her work ethic.

There is so much in that paragraph alone. In order for your business to flourish you must have integrity, do not be willing to compromise for the sake of worldly gain and be willing to be uncomfortable at times. Familiar things and places are not what's going to pay off because growth takes places when we are willing to move. Ruth was determined to go a different path when Naomi said she was returning home.

Businesses with integrity exhibits values: honesty, sincerity, trust, reliability, kindness, compassion, and respect. In addition, your customers will love you for it. Here are four things you should do:
1. **Provide a quality service or product-** Ask yourself would you use your product or service. This will ensure you have a business you can be proud to talk about.
2. **Keep your promise-** Do what you say you are going to do!
3. **Deal with mistakes-** There will be mistakes so don't get anxiety. The best thing to do is be honest about any mistakes. Acknowledge and learn from them and implement any changes so the mistakes won't be repeated. Remember, how you respond to mistakes determines your outcome.
4. **Do the right thing-** Especially when no one is looking! Why? Because integrity is what you do when no one is looking. No matter what the circumstance, always do what you know in your heart to be the right thing. Customers and clients will notice your integrity when you are always doing what is right. Being a person who is valued for their integrity goes a long way in business as well as in your personal life.

Now that we have discussed integrity, let us talk about vision. Ruth had to have vision in order to leave with Naomi and she had to see herself out there in the fields working. You may have saw her as just working in the fields, but remember I said to look at her from the position of an independent contractor.

VISION- is a mental image of the future you desire, and you cannot build a business without a clear vision. A vision is the embodiment of our hopes and dreams; the picture of what has not yet happened, but what the future may hold.

"The future belongs to those who see possibilities before they become obvious." - John Scully

This is a good place to define and write your vision. Remember to be *specific*, be *positive* and be *ambitious*. A good vision sets a degree of excellence, distinction, performance, and it compels your business to stretch.

PERSONAL VISION:

_____
_____
_____
_____
_____
_____

BUSINESS VISION:

_____
_____
_____
_____
_____
_____

Now that we have discussed vision, let talk about a business coach and why they are important to grow your business.

BUSINESS COACH- A business coach is an advisor that provides an outside perspective for you and your business. This is someone who helps you move from where you are to where you want to be and does so by focusing on your goals.

Coaching is unlocking a person's potential to maximize their growth. -Unknown (Honestly credit was given to more than one person, so I chose to say unknown)

A business coach can provide you with unbiased feedback and new innovative ideas. In today's business it can be tough and if nothing else competitive. Things are changing and what you did yesterday may not work for today and a business coach can assist you with staying on top of the newest business trends.

Always be open to learning and developing new skills. Life is all about change and if you are not changing, your business will definitely be left behind. I read a book recently called, *'Who Moved My Cheese'* by Spencer Johnson, this was a very enlightening book, and it will help you understand why you must change and be open to new things, especially in business.

We all need help at some point in our lives and businesses run better when we have others assisting. Let's be honest, we cannot do everything ourselves and have a productive business, something will get overlooked. A great business coach can help you push beyond those self-perceived limits.

Many famous people have used some form of coaching to take their skills or their businesses to that next level. Some examples are Oprah Winfrey, Former President Obama, Tiger Woods, Serena Williams, just to name a few.

This is a suitable place to research some business coaches or at least get with someone that can give you an outside perspective for your business. Now write down a few names.

1. _____

2. _____

3. _____

4. _____

5. _____

I gave you five (5) lines in case you needed to add a personal coach. *(Smile)*

You're probably thinking I got away from Ruth, but I didn't. Naomi was that advisor who provided an outside perspective for her, a sort of mentorship for Ruth.

Then Naomi said to her, "My daughter, shall I not seek security for you, that it may be well with you?"

The first step is understanding the basics of how you're going to run your business, which means making a plan that outlines all facets of how you will function day to day. This will help you avoid many mistakes and give you the assurance that you have everything covered.

As a female, we tend to take on many different task and it's no secret that starting a small business often call for you to wear many different hats. Being flexible is one thing, but doing everything is not good for business. It is important to know what skills you have, what skills you are willing to delegate and which ones you are willing to learn.

I mention in the introduction that the village is important in our businesses because we need to be reminded at times that we cannot do it all and be successful. You're probably saying, "I really can do it all." The key here is...AND BE SUCCESSFUL.

You will get worn out, overwhelmed and you won't be able to give your client/customer 100% which will cause your business to fail.

Be strong enough to stand-alone
Smart enough to know when you need help
Brave enough to ask for it
—Ziad Abdelnour

NOTES

A friend of mine asked recently, *"How can I become a successful female entrepreneur?"*

My immediate response was, *'You need to renew your mind. Don't become so well-adjusted to your culture that you fit into it without even thinking."* I study the Word of G-d, so the Word just seems to flow right out of me, but success in business is extremely reliant on the mindset.

You also should **believe in who you are and what you can do**, even if no one else does. As a woman, we tend to underestimate our abilities and skills. If you lack self-confidence, it will show when you are talking about your product or service. So, develop the confidence that you have something valuable inside of you.

Ask yourself this question, *'Why do I want to become an entrepreneur?'* This question may seem simple but it a component that establishes whether you will succeed or fail as an entrepreneur. Let me ask that again: *what is your reason for starting a business*? I want you to keep in mind that building a successful business begins with the *'why.'*

This is a suitable place to write your '***Why***':

_____
_____
_____
_____
_____

NOTES

BE OPEN TO CRITICISM. The ability to process criticism and grow from it is particularly important to the success of your business. However, know there are two different forms of criticism and there is a difference between them. You need to learn how to recognize them.

Constructive criticism is feedback to help you to improve and should be regarded as positive. The main feature of constructive criticism is that it is an objective assessment. Constructive criticism does not hurt the individual or tear down self-esteem. It helps the person to perform better once they are aware of the mistakes.

Destructive criticism, nonetheless, is feedback intended to hurt your self-esteem, make you feel hurt or even angry. It is not intended to help you or allow you to see what you did wrong and improve on it.

And she said to her, "All that you say to me I will do." So she went down to the threshing floor and did according to all that her mother-in-law instructed her.

FOLLOW YOUR PASSION. It is much more effortless to motivate yourself to do the work when you're excited about what you're doing. Working towards something you're enthusiastic about will give you drive during the difficult times and fulfillment during the good.

If you are not sure about your passion, don't worry not everyone can identify a particular passion, it may take some time. Consider an appointment with a career coach to help you recognize your strengths and weaknesses and gain a sharper vision of your business goals.

MARKETING IS KEY. Every business, regardless of size, will need a brand. A brand is more than a logo, color, or tagline. A well-communicated brand passionately hits it off with your intended customers and publicizes who you are, what you stand for and what you can deliver.

Promoting your product or service to everyone can be pricey and unproductive. Categorizing your possible customers/clients based on certain characteristics will help to focus your marketing energies. Your target market should have a need for your product or service and be willing to pay for your offer.

MANAGEMENT. It is what allows you to anticipate upcoming situations and organize things needed. Without skilled management, everything else falls because your business would have no direction.

Basic business strategy is essential for starting entrepreneurs, it allows you to think carefully before any action and act according to any situation. Strategic thinking, along with practical thinking, is important for your business to grow, last long, and expand.

QUALITY OVER QUANTITY. Quality is one of the most vital things when it comes to the basics of business. Customers will always choose quality over quantity 10 times out of ten. It is important to ensure that your products or services are top quality.

ONLINE MARKETING. Social media and online selling offers opportunities for starting businesses. This is largely because the today's world is dependent on the use of the internet to browse about particular needs and wants.

Do you know what a **USP** is? It stands for **Unique Selling Proposition**. A unique selling proposition represents what your business stands for. It is that quality about your business that sets it apart from the competition. It is the reason your customers buy from you and not your competitors. It is important to define what you do differently and be able to convey that to potential customers.

Start improving your USP by answering the following questions:

1. What specific skills or knowledge do you have to offer?

   _____
   _____
   _____
   _____

2. How do your customers benefit by purchasing your products or services?

   _____
   _____
   _____
   _____

3. What makes your customers come to you instead of your competitors?

   _____
   _____
   _____
   _____

4. How do you describe your business to potential customers?

_____
_____
_____
_____

5. What do YOU love most about your products/service?

_____
_____
_____
_____

Marketing goals will help you to define what you want to achieve through your marketing activities. Your goals should be **SMART**:

Specific-Focused and well defined.
Measurable-Numbers are essential in business.
Achievable-Dream big but keep one foot firmly in reality.
Reasonable-Goals based on current conditions.
Time-based-Set a timeframe on the goal-setting process.

You should monitor and review your marketing activities to establish whether they are reaching the desired outcome, such as increased sales. It is good to review your marketing plan every three months to ensure your activities are sustaining your strategy. Once your business is in good standing review your plan when you introduce a new product or service, if a new competitor enters the market or if an issue occurs that influences your industry.

NOTES

NOTES

BUSINESS CHECKLIST

1. **Select a Name and Legal Structure**
   Sole Proprietorship
   Partnership
   Limited Liability Company (LLC)
   Corporation or S-Corporation

2. **Write a Business Plan**
   Prepare at least a preliminary business plan.

3. **Obtain an Employer Identification Number (EIN)**
   Apply for an Employer Identification Number (EIN) from the IRS. An EIN will be necessary to open a bank account or process payroll.

4. **Open a Business Account**
   Select a bank and open the company bank account. Do your due diligence to find out which bank fits your business and what type of fees they have.

5. **If not Home-Based, Locate a Workspace**
   Depending on your type of business, arrange for office space to be leased. Contacting a commercial realtor in your area can be helpful. Also, make sure to arrange for utilities and office furniture.

6. **Obtain Licenses and Permits (if needed)**
   Depending on the type of business you are in, you may or may not need a federal license or permit.

7. **Hire Employees (if applicable)**
   You may have to register with the appropriate State Agencies or obtain Workers Compensation Insurance or Unemployment Insurance (or both).

8. **Set up Accounting or Record-Keeping System**
   Learn about the taxes your new company is responsible for paying.

9. **Obtain Business Insurance (if needed)**
   There are many types of insurance for businesses, but they are usually packaged as "General Business Insurance" or a "Business Owner's Policy." This can cover everything from product liability to company vehicles.

10. **Systemize and Organize**
    Make the operational aspect of the business as automated and efficient as possible so you can concentrate on growing your business.

11. **Develop a Business Identity**
    Order business cards, letterhead, and promotional materials for your business. A professionally created logo can make your business look professional and established.

12. **Get the Word Out**
    Now that you have set-up the company for success, you need to get the word out. Create a marketing plan for your products and services that targets your ideal customer.

FIVE TAX TIPS
Please make sure you contact your tax professional

You can claim startup tax deductions for eligible expenses:

The IRS allows you **to deduct up to $5,000 in business startup costs** and up to $5,000 in organizational costs, but only if your total startup costs are $50,000 or less. With the help of your tax software or a tax expert, you can write off typical costs associated with setting up a business during tax filing.

1. HOME OFFICE/UTILITIES

Since this is a relatively new tax deduction, it was permitted in 2013; it is not surprising that most entrepreneurs aren't familiar with it. The home office deduction allows small businesses that operate out of a home to deduct for every square foot of space used for the business, up to 300 square feet."

If you're taking a home office deduction, then you can also deduct a portion of your utility bill. In most cases, this applies to your monthly heating and electricity bills. You should also be able to claim your internet and phone use.

2. OFFICE SUPPLIES

How about all of the paper, ink toner, postage, and paper clips that you've purchased? Yep, this is one of the best business tax tips. They are all fully deductible – provided you can prove its being used for business.

How about that shiny new computer or iPad? These items can also be deducted. However, if you are using the same computer or tablet for personal and business use, then you can only deduct the percentage of how often the equipment is used for business.

3. TRAVEL EXPENSES

How about those business trips? Everything from airfare, lodging, dry cleaning, and even 50 percent of your meals is fair game. Even renting essential work related equipment and the cost of entertaining prospective clients could be claimed.

4. MILEAGE

All those rides going to the airport or to other cafes meeting clients. Yes. In addition to reporting the income (Form 1099), you may be able to deduct business mileage – even if you used your personal vehicle.

5. LUNCH

This is a long-standing tradition but it's also one of everyone's favorite business tax tips. It can also get a little confusing for most business owners so make sure you consult with your tax professional.

You can only deduct 50 percent of the meal. Additionally, the meal cannot be extravagant. For example, flying your client to New York City and dropping a grand for lunch is a no-no.

There are a whole lot more tax tips so make sure you communicate with your tax professional.

NOTES

NOTES

NOTES

NOTES

NOTES

NOTES

NOTES

NOTES

NOTES

www.ingramcontent.com/pod-product-compliance
Lightning Source LLC
Chambersburg PA
CBHW030044230526
45472CB00005B/1663